M000207819

PSALMS FOR
CHRISTIAN PRAYER

PSALMS FOR CHRISTIAN PRAYER

Bede Griffiths

Edited by
Roland R. Ropers

HarperCollins*Publishers*

HarperCollins*Publishers*
77–85 Fulham Palace Road, London W6 8JB

First published in Great Britain
in 1995 by HarperCollins*Publishers*

1 3 5 7 9 10 8 6 4 2

Copyright © 1995 by Bede Griffiths

A catalogue record for this book is
available from the British Library

ISBN 0 00 627956 2

Printed and bound in Great Britain by
HarperCollinsManufacturing Glasgow

CONTENTS

INTRODUCTION

From the earliest times the songs of the Hebrew Psalter have been held in veneration by the Christian Church. They were considered to have been inspired by God and to have been the prayer of Jesus himself. St Benedict in his Rule was careful to arrange for the whole Psalter to be sung every week in choir, and declared that the 'holy fathers were wont to recite in a single day what we tepid monks may only sing in a week'. If there were any problems about the sentiments expressed in some of the Psalms, the difficulty was overcome by interpreting them in an 'allegorical' sense. The model for this kind of interpretation can be found in St Augustine's commentary on the Psalms, in which the Psalms are conceived to be the inspired utterance of Christ himself speaking as Head of his mystical body, the Church. There is no doubt about the deep significance of the Psalms when interpreted in this way, but it is done at the expense of their literal meaning, the 'enemies' of the Psalmist being conceived as evil spirits who war against the Christian. This symbolic understanding has been continued until the present day, but as we come to attend more closely to the literal meaning of the Psalms, which for an educated person today is almost inevitable, it becomes more and more difficult to accept many of them as Christian prayers. Taken in their literal sense many of the Psalms express feelings of anger, hatred and revenge against one's enemies which are entirely opposed to the teaching of the Gospel on love of one's enemies, and the habit of labelling a whole class of one's fellowmen as 'enemies', and 'wicked' and 'sinners' is intolerable for anyone who has been taught to 'love one's neighbours as oneself'.

What is perhaps even more unacceptable, the same sentiments of anger, hatred and revenge are attributed to God himself, and the Messiah in the famous Messianic Psalms (2 and 109) is depicted as a king who will conquer and destroy his enemies, trampling them under his feet. 'He will rule them with a rod of iron' and 'break them in pieces like a potter's vessel'. In this the Messiah is shown to be the very opposite of Jesus Christ who allowed his enemies to crush him and came not to destroy but to save. It has become urgent, therefore, to revise the Psalter, so that all branding of others as 'enemies', 'wicked' and 'sinners' deserving no mercy or pity should be removed. When one considers the incalculable harm which has resulted from this habit of mind in the Church as seen in the Inquisition, the Crusades, the wars of religion and the persecution of 'heretics', it is clear that a revision of this kind is urgently needed.

We have to remember that ancient Israel grew up in a dualistic culture in which God was considered to be

separate – the word 'holy' originally meant separate –
from humanity and the created world. Human beings
were separate from God and one another and from the
surrounding world. Israel was a 'holy' nation separate
from the other nations of the world. As a result Israel
was surrounded by 'enemies', who were hostile to God
and to the people of God. The good were separate from
the 'wicked', the righteous from sinners, and the end
was conceived to be the destruction of the 'wicked' and
all the 'enemies' of Israel. The Messiah was to conquer
their enemies and subdue them under his feet. This was
the perspective of the Psalmist and it was precisely this
dualism which Jesus came to overcome. He 'broke
down the dividing wall' between Jews and Gentiles. He
came not to conquer and subdue his enemies but to
save them and reconcile them with God. He came to
save not the 'righteous' but sinners, to 'seek and save
that which was lost'. Thus the whole perspective of the
Psalms was reversed and to continue to use the Psalms
in their literal sense is to perpetuate what Jesus came to
bring to an end. There is, however, another side to the
tradition of Israel, a sense of universalism, a longing
for peace and reconciliation, a recognition of the mercy
and grace of God towards sinners. These Psalms still
retain their value and can be used in Christian prayer.
We can praise God for all the work of creation, thank
him for his providence over human life, ask for mercy
and forgiveness and look forward to the joy of reconciliation and union with God. These Psalms retain all

their values for Christian prayer when they have been separated from every suggestion of anger, hatred and revenge and can be seen to lead to reconciliation in Christ of all humanity and the whole creation.

Bede Griffiths
Shantigiri (Mount of Peace)
Kreuth, Tegernsee
Germany
March 1992

THE PSALMS

4

When I call, answer me, O God of justice;
from anguish you released me, have mercy and hear
    me.

O men, how long will your hearts be closed,
will you love what is futile and seek what is false?

It is the Lord who grants favours to those whom he
    loves;
the Lord hears me whenever I call him.

Fear him; do not sin; ponder on your bed and be still.
Make justice your sacrifice and trust in the Lord.

'What can bring us happiness?' many say.
Lift up the light of your face on us, O Lord.

You have put into my heart a greater joy
than they have from abundance of corn and new wine.

I will lie down in peace and sleep comes at once
for you alone, Lord, make me dwell in safety.

8

How great is your name, O Lord our God,
through all the earth!

Your majesty is praised above the heavens;
on the lips of children and of babes
you have found praise.

When I see the heavens, the work of your hands,
the moon and the stars which you arranged,
what is man that you should keep him in mind,
mortal man that you care for him?

Yet you have made him little less than a God;
with glory and honour you crowned him,
gave him power over the works of your hand,
put all things under his feet.

All of them, sheep and cattle,
yes, even the savage beasts,
birds of the air, and fish
that make their way through the waters.

How great is your name, O Lord our God,
through all the earth!

15 (16)*

Preserve me, God, I take refuge in you.
I say to the Lord: 'You are my God.
My happiness lies in you alone.'

He has put into my heart a marvellous love
for the faithful ones who dwell in his land.

O Lord, it is you who are my portion and cup;
it is you yourself who are my prize.
The lot marked out for me is my delight:
welcome indeed the heritage that falls to me!

I will bless the Lord who gives me counsel,
who even at night directs my heart.
I keep the Lord ever in my sight:
since he is at my right hand, I shall stand firm.

And so my heart rejoices, my soul is glad:
even my body shall rest in safety.
For you will not leave my soul among the dead,
nor let your beloved know decay.

You will show me the path of life,
the fullness of joy in your presence,
at your right hand happiness for ever.

* The numbering of the Psalms is taken from the Douay Version of the Bible.
The figures in brackets are the King James Version Psalm numbers.

18 (19)

The heavens proclaim the glory of God
and the firmament shows forth the work of his hands.
Day unto day takes up the story
and night unto night makes known the message.

No speech, no word, no voice is heard
yet their span goes forth through all the earth,
their words to the utmost bounds of the world.

There he has placed a tent for the sun;
it comes forth like a bridegroom coming from his tent,
rejoices like a champion to run its course.

At the end of the sky is the rising of the sun;
to the furthest end of the sky is its course.
There is nothing concealed from its burning heat.

✳

The law of the Lord is perfect,
it revives the soul.
The rule of the Lord is to be trusted,
it gives wisdom to the simple.

The precepts of the Lord are right,
they gladden the heart.
The command of the Lord is clear,
it gives light to the eyes.

The fear of the Lord is holy,
abiding for ever.
The decrees of the Lord are truth
and all of them just.

They are more to be desired than gold,
than the purest of gold
and sweeter are they than honey,
than honey from the comb.

So in them your servant finds instruction;
great reward is in their keeping.
But who can detect all his errors?
From hidden faults acquit me.

From presumption restrain your servant
and let it not rule me.
Then shall I be blameless,
clean from grave sin.

May the spoken words of my mouth,
the thoughts of my heart,
win favour in your sight, O Lord,
my rescuer, my rock!

22 (23)

The Lord is my shepherd;
there is nothing I shall want.
Fresh and green are the pastures
where he gives me repose.
Near restful waters he leads me,
to revive my drooping spirit.

He guides me along the right path;
he is true to his name.
If I should walk in the valley of darkness
no evil would I fear.
You are there with your crook and your staff;
with these you give me comfort.

My head you have anointed with oil;
my cup is overflowing.

Surely goodness and kindness shall follow me
all the days of my life.
In the Lord's own house shall I dwell
for ever and ever.

26 (27)

The Lord is my light and my help;
whom shall I fear?
The Lord is the stronghold of my life;
before whom shall I shrink?

Though an army encamp against me
my heart would not fear.
Though war break out against me
even then would I trust.

There is one thing I ask of the Lord,
for this I long,
to live in the house of the Lord
all the days of my life,
to savour the sweetness of the Lord,
to behold his temple.

For there he keeps me safe in his tent
in the day of evil.
He hides me in the shelter of his tent,
on a rock sets me safe.

And now my head shall be raised
and I shall offer within his tent
a sacrifice of joy.

I will sing and make music for the Lord.

O Lord, hear my voice when I call;
have mercy and answer.
Of you my heart has spoken:
'Seek his face.'

It is your face, O Lord, that I seek;
hide not your face.

Dismiss not your servant in anger;
you have been my help.

Do not abandon or forsake me,
O God my help!
Though father and mother forsake me,
the Lord will receive me.

Instruct me, Lord, in your way;
on an even path lead me.

I am sure I shall see the Lord's goodness
in the land of the living.
Hope in him, hold firm and take heart.
Hope in the Lord!

28 (29)

O give the Lord, you sons of God,
give the Lord glory and power;
give the Lord the glory of his name.
Adore the Lord in his holy court.

The Lord's voice resounding on the waters,
the Lord on the immensity of waters;
the voice of the Lord, full of power,
the voice of the Lord, full of splendour.

The Lord's voice shattering the cedars,
the Lord shatters the cedars of Lebanon;
he makes Lebanon leap like a calf
and Sirion like a young wild-ox.

(The Lord's voice flashes flames of fire.)

The Lord's voice shattering the wilderness,
the Lord shakes the wilderness of Kadesh;
the Lord's voice rending the oak tree
and stripping the forest bare.

The God of glory thunders.
In his temple they all cry: 'Glory!'
The Lord sat enthroned over the flood;
the Lord sits as king for ever.

The Lord will give strength to his people,
the Lord will bless his people with peace.

31 (32)

Happy the man whose offence is forgiven,
whose sin is remitted.
O happy the man to whom the Lord
imputes no guilt,
in whose spirit is no guile.

I kept it secret and my frame was wasted.
I groaned all the day long
for night and day your hand
was heavy upon me.
Indeed, my strength was dried up
as by the summer's heat.

But now I have acknowledged my sins;
my guilt I did not hide.
I said: 'I will confess
my offence to the Lord.'
And you, Lord, have forgiven
the guilt of my sin.

So let every good man pray to you
in the time of need.
The floods of water may reach high
but him they shall not reach.
You are my hiding place, O Lord;
you save me from distress.
(You surround me with cries of deliverance.)

I will instruct you and teach you
the way you should go;
I will give you counsel
with my eye upon you.

Be not like horse and mule, unintelligent,
needing bridle and bit,
else they will not approach you.
He who trusts in the Lord,
loving mercy surrounds him.

Rejoice, rejoice in the Lord,
exult, you just!
O come, ring out your joy,
all you upright of heart.

32 (33)

Ring out your joy to the Lord, O you just;
for praise is fitting for loyal hearts.

Give thanks to the Lord upon the harp,
with a ten-stringed lute sing him songs.
O sing him a song that is new,
play loudly, with all your skill.

For the word of the Lord is faithful
and all his works to be trusted.
The Lord loves justice and right
and fills the earth with his love.

By his word the heavens were made,
by the breath of his mouth all the stars.
He collects the waves of the ocean;
he stores up the depths of the sea.

Let all the earth fear the Lord,
all who live in the world revere him.
He spoke; and it came to be.
He commanded; it sprang into being.

His own designs shall stand for ever,
the plans of his heart from age to age.

They are happy, whose God is the Lord,
the people he has chosen as his own.
From the heavens the Lord looks forth,
he sees all the children of men.

From the place where he dwells he gazes
on all the dwellers on the earth,
he who shapes the hearts of them all
and considers all their deeds.

A king is not saved by his army,
nor a warrior preserved by his strength.
A vain hope for safety is the horse;
despite its power it cannot save.

The Lord looks on those who revere him,
on those who hope in his love,
to rescue their souls from death,
to keep them alive in famine.

Our soul is waiting for the Lord.
The Lord is our help and our shield.
In him do our hearts find joy.
We trust in his holy name.

May your love be upon us, O Lord,
as we place all our hope in you.

33 (34)

I will bless the Lord at all times,
his praise always on my lips;
in the Lord my soul shall make its boast.
The humble shall hear and be glad.

Glorify the Lord with me.
Together let us praise his name.
I sought the Lord and he answered me;
from all my terrors he set me free.

Look towards him and be radiant;
let your faces not be abashed.
This poor man called; the Lord heard him
and rescued him from all his distress.

The angel of the Lord is encamped
around those who revere him, to rescue them.
Taste and see that the Lord is good.
He is happy who seeks refuge in him.

Revere the Lord, you his saints.
They lack nothing, those who revere him.
Strong lions suffer want and go hungry;
but those who seek the Lord lack no blessing.

Come children, and hear me;
that I may teach you the fear of the Lord.

Who is he who longs for life
and many days, to enjoy his prosperity?

Then keep your tongue from evil
and your lips from speaking deceit.
Turn aside from evil and do good;
seek and strive after peace.

The Lord turns his eyes to the just
and his ears to their appeal.

They call and the Lord hears
and rescues them in all their distress.
The Lord is close to the broken-hearted;
those whose spirit is crushed he will save.

Many are the trials of the just man:
but from them all the Lord will rescue him.
He will keep guard over all his bones:
not one of his bones shall be broken.

The Lord ransoms the souls of his servants.
Those who hide in him shall not be condemned.

35 (36)

Your love, Lord, reaches to heaven;
your truth to the skies.
Your justice is like God's mountain,
your judgments like the deep.

To both man and beast you give protection.
O Lord, how precious is your love.
My God, the sons of men
find refuge in the shelter of your wings.

They feast on the riches of your house;
they drink from the stream of your delight.
In you is the source of life
and in your light we see light.

Keep on loving those who know you,
doing justice for upright hearts.

39 (40)

I waited, I waited for the Lord,
and he stooped down to me;
he heard my cry.

He drew me from the deadly pit,
from the miry clay.
He set my feet upon a rock
and made my footsteps firm.

He put a new song into my mouth,
praise of our God.
Many shall see and fear
and shall trust in the Lord.

Happy the man who has placed
his trust in the Lord.

How many, O Lord my God,
are the wonders and designs
that you have worked for us;
you have no equal.
Should I proclaim and speak of them,
they are more than I can tell!
You do not ask for sacrifice and offerings,
but an open ear.
You do not ask for holocaust and victim.
Instead, here am I.

In the scroll of the Book it stands written
that I should do your will.
My God, I delight in your law
in the depth of my heart.

Your justice I have proclaimed
in the great assembly.
My lips I have not sealed;
you know it, O Lord.

I have not hidden your justice in my heart,
but declared your faithful help.
I have not hidden your love and your truth
from the great assembly.

O Lord, you will not withhold
your compassion from me.
Your merciful love and your truth
will always guard me.

For I am beset with evils
too many to be counted.
My sins have fallen upon me
and my sight fails me.
They are more than the hairs of my head
and my heart sinks.

O Lord, come to my rescue,
Lord, come to my aid.

O let there be rejoicing and gladness
for all who seek you.
Let them ever say: 'The Lord is great',
who love your saving help.

As for me, wretched and poor,
the Lord thinks of me.
You are my rescuer, my help,
O God, do not delay.

41 (42)

Like the deer that yearns
for running streams,
so my soul is yearning
for you, my God.

My soul is thirsting for God,
the God of my life;
when can I enter and see
the face of God?

My tears have become my bread,
by night, by day,
as I hear it said all the day long:
'Where is your God?'

These things will I remember
as I pour out my soul:
how I would lead the rejoicing crowd
into the house of God,
amid cries of gladness and thanksgiving,
the throng wild with joy.

Why are you cast down, my soul,
why groan within me?
Hope in God; I will praise him still,
my saviour and my God.

My soul is cast down within me
as I think of you,
from the country of Jordan and Mount Hermon,
from the Hill of Mizar.

Deep is calling on deep,
in the roar of waters:
your torrents and all your waves
swept over me.

By day the Lord will send
his loving kindness;
by night I will sing to him,
praise the God of my life.

Why are you cast down, my soul,
why groan within me?
Hope in God; I will praise him still,
my saviour and my God.

45 (46)

God is for us a refuge and strength,
a helper close at hand, in time of distress:
so we shall not fear though the earth should rock,
though the mountains fall into the depths of the sea,
even though its waters rage and foam,
even though the mountains be shaken by its waves.

The Lord of hosts is with us:
The God of Jacob is our stronghold.

The waters of a river give joy to God's city,
The holy place where the Most High dwells.
God is within, it cannot be shaken;
God will help it at the dawning of the day.
Nations are in tumult, kingdoms are shaken:
he lifts his voice, the earth shrinks away.

The Lord of hosts is with us:
The God of Jacob is our stronghold.

Come, consider the works of the Lord,
The redoubtable deeds he has done on the earth.
He puts an end to wars over all the earth;
the bow he breaks, the spear he snaps.
He burns the shields with fire.
'Be still and know that I am God,
supreme among the nations, supreme on the earth!'

The Lord of hosts is with us:
the God of Jacob is our stronghold.

46 (47)

All peoples, clap your hands,
cry to God with shouts of joy!
For the Lord, the Most High, we must fear,
great king over all the earth.

Our inheritance, our glory, is from him,
given to Jacob out of love.

God goes up with shouts of joy;
the Lord goes up with trumpet blast.
Sing praise to God, sing praise,
sing praise to our king, sing praise.

God is king of all the earth.
Sing praise with all your skill.
God is king over the nations;
God reigns on his holy throne.

The princes of the peoples are assembled
with the people of Abraham's God.
The rulers of the earth belong to God,
to God who reigns over all.

50 (51)

Have mercy on me, God, in your kindness.
In your compassion blot out my offence.
O wash me more and more from my guilt
and cleanse me from my sin.

My offences truly I know them;
my sin is always before me.
Against you, you alone, have I sinned;
what is evil in your sight I have done.

That you may be justified when you give sentence
and be without reproach when you judge,
O see, in guilt I was born,
a sinner was I conceived.

Indeed you love truth in the heart;
then in the secret of my heart teach me wisdom.
O purify me, then I shall be clean;
O wash me, I shall be whiter than snow.

Make me hear rejoicing and gladness,
that the bones you have crushed may thrill.
From my sins turn away your face
and blot out all my guilt.

A pure heart create for me, O God,
put a steadfast spirit within me.
Do not cast me away from your presence,
nor deprive me of your holy spirit.

Give me again the joy of your help;
with a spirit of fervour sustain me,
that I may teach transgressors your ways
and sinners may return to you.

O rescue me God, my helper,
and my tongue shall ring out your goodness.
O Lord, open my lips
and my mouth shall declare your praise.

For in sacrifice you take no delight,
burnt offering from me you would refuse.
My sacrifice, a contrite spirit.
A humbled, contrite heart you will not spurn.

56 (57)

Have mercy on me, God have mercy:
for in you my soul has taken refuge.
In the shadow of your wings I take refuge
till the storms of destruction pass by.

I call to God the Most High,
to God who has always been my help.
May he send from heaven and save me.
May God send his truth and his love.

O God, arise above the heavens;
may your glory shine on earth!

My heart is ready, O God,
my heart is ready.
I will sing, I will sing your praise.
Awake lyre and harp,
I will awake the dawn.

Praise you among the nations;
I will thank you, Lord, among the nations;
for your love reaches to the heavens
and your truth to the skies.

O God, arise above the heavens;
may your glory shine on earth!

60 (61)

O God, hear my cry!
Listen to my prayer!
From the end of the earth I call:
my heart is faint.

On the rock too high for me to reach
set me on high,
O you who have been my refuge,
my tower against the foe.

Let me dwell in your tent for ever
and hide in the shelter of your wings.
For you, O God, hear my prayer
and grant me the heritage of those who fear you.

May you lengthen the life of the king:
may his years cover many generations.
May he ever sit enthroned before God:
bid love and truth be his protection.

So I will always praise your name
and day after day fulfil my vows.

61 (62)

In God alone is my soul at rest;
my help comes from him.
He alone is my rock, my stronghold,
my fortress: I stand firm.

How long will you all attack one man
to break him down,
as though he were a tottering wall,
or a tumbling fence?

In God alone be at rest, my soul;
for my hope comes from him.
He alone is my rock, my stronghold,
my fortress: I stand firm.

In God is my safety and glory,
the rock of my strength.
Take refuge in God all you people.
Trust him at all times.
Pour out your hearts before him
for God is our refuge.

Common folk are only a breath,
great men an illusion.
Placed in the scales, they rise;
they weigh less than a breath.

Do not put your trust in oppression
nor vain hopes on plunder.
Do not set your heart on riches
even when they increase.

For God has said only one thing:
only two do I know:
that to God alone belongs power
and to you, Lord, love.

62 (63)

O God, you are my God, for you I long;
for you my soul is thirsting.
My body pines for you
like a dry, weary land without water.
So I gaze on you in the sanctuary
to see your strength and your glory.

For your love is better than life,
my lips will speak your praise.
So I will bless you all my life,
in your name I will lift up my hands.
My soul shall be filled as with a banquet,
my mouth shall praise you with joy.

On my bed I remember you.
On you I muse through the night
for you have been my help;
in the shadow of your wings I rejoice.
My soul clings to you;
your right hand holds me fast.

64 (65)

To you our praise is due
in Sion, O God.
To you we pay our vows,
you who hear our prayer.

To you all flesh will come
with its burden of sin.
Too heavy for us, our offences,
but you wipe them away.

Blessed he whom you choose and call
to dwell in your courts.
We are filled with the blessings of your house,
of your holy temple.

You keep your pledge with wonders,
O God our saviour,
the hope of all the earth
and of far distant isles.

You uphold the mountains with your strength,
you are girded with power.
You still the roaring of the seas
(the roaring of their waves)
and the tumult of the peoples.

The ends of the earth stand in awe
at the sight of your wonders.
The lands of sunrise and sunset
you fill with your joy.

You care for the earth, give it water,
you fill it with riches.
Your river in heaven brims over
to provide its grain.

And thus you provide for the earth;
you drench its furrows,
you level it, soften it with showers,
you bless its growth.

You crown the year with your goodness.
Abundance flows in your steps,
in the pastures of the wilderness it flows.

The hills are girded with joy,
the meadows covered with flocks,
the valleys are decked with wheat.
They shout for joy, yes, they sing.

65 (66)

Cry out with joy to God all the earth,
O sing to the glory of his name.
O render him glorious praise.
Say to God: 'How tremendous your deeds!
Before you all the earth shall bow;
shall sing to you, sing to your name!'

Come and see the works of God,
tremendous his deeds among men.
He turned the sea into dry land,
they passed through the river dry-shod.

Let our joy then be in him;
he rules for ever by his might.
His eyes keep watch over the nations:
let rebels not rise against him.

O peoples, bless our God,
let the voice of his praise resound,
of the God who gave life to our souls
and kept our feet from stumbling.

For you, O God, have tested us,
you have tried us as silver is tried:
you led us, God, into the snare;
you laid a heavy burden on our backs.

You let men ride over our heads;
we went through fire and through water
but then you brought us relief.

Burnt offering I bring to your house;
to you I will pay my vows,
the vows which my lips have uttered,
which my mouth spoke in my distress.

Come and hear, all who fear God.
I will tell what he did for my soul;
to him I cried aloud,
with high praise ready on my tongue.

If there had been evil in my heart,
the Lord would not have listened.
But truly God has listened;
he has heeded the voice of my prayer.

Blessed be God who did not reject my prayer
nor withhold his love from me.

66 (67)

O God, be gracious and bless us
and let your face shed its light upon us.
So will your ways be known upon earth
and all nations learn your saving help.

Let the peoples praise you, O God;
let all the peoples praise you.

Let the nations be glad and exult,
for you rule the world with justice.
With fairness you rule the peoples,
you guide the nations on earth.

Let the peoples praise you, O God;
let all the peoples praise you.

The earth has yielded its fruit,
for God, our God, has blessed us.
May God still give us his blessing
till the ends of the earth revere him.

Let the peoples praise you, O God;
let all the peoples praise you.

67 (68)

The just shall rejoice at the presence of God,
they shall exult and dance for joy.
O sing to the Lord, make music to his name;
make a highway for him who rides on the clouds.
Rejoice in the Lord, exult at his presence.

Father of the orphan, defender of the widow,
such is God in his holy place.
God gives the lonely a home to live in;
he leads the prisoner forth into freedom:
but rebels must dwell in a parched land.

When you went forth, O God, at the head of your
    people,
when you marched across the desert, the earth trembled:
the heavens melted at the presence of God,
at the presence of God, Israel's God.

You poured down, O God, a generous rain:
when your people were starved you gave them new life.
It was there that your people found a home,
prepared in your goodness, O God, for the poor.

May the Lord be blessed day after day.
He bears our burdens, God our saviour.
This God of ours is a God who saves.
The Lord our God holds the keys of death.

They see your solemn procession, O God,
the procession of my God, of my king, to the sanctuary:
the singers in the forefront, the musicians coming last,
between them, maidens sounding their timbrels.

'In festive gatherings, bless the Lord;
bless God, O you who are Israel's sons.'
There is Benjamin, least of the tribes, at the head,
Judah's princes, a mighty throng,
Zebulun's princes, Naphtali's princes.

Kingdoms of the earth, sing to God, praise the Lord
who rides on the heavens, the ancient heavens.
He thunders his voice, his mighty voice.
Come, acknowledge the power of God.

His glory is over Israel; his might is in the skies.
God is to be feared in his holy place.
He is the Lord, Israel's God.
He gives strength and power to his people.

Blessed be God!

68 (69)

Save me, O God,
for the waters have risen to my neck.

I have sunk into the mud of the deep
and there is no foothold.
I have entered the waters of the deep
and the waves overwhelm me.

I am wearied with all my crying,
my throat is parched.
My eyes are wasted away
from looking for my God.

How can I restore
what I have never stolen?
O God, you know my sinful folly;
my sins you can see.

Let not those who hope in you be put to shame
through me, Lord of hosts:
let not those who seek you be dismayed
through me, God of Israel.

It is for you that I suffer taunts,
that shame covers my face,
that I have become a stranger to my brothers,
an alien to my own mother's sons.

I burn with zeal for your house
and taunts against you fall on me.

When I afflict my soul with fasting
they make it a taunt against me.
When I put on sackcloth in mourning
then they make me a byword,
the gossip of men at the gates,
the subject of drunkards' songs.

This is my prayer to you,
my prayer for your favour.
In your great love, answer me, O God,
with your help that never fails:
rescue me from sinking in the mud;
save me from my foes.

Save me from the waters of the deep
lest the wave overwhelm me.
Do not let the deep engulf me
nor death close its mouth on me.

Lord, answer, for your love is kind;
in your compassion, turn towards me.
Do not hide your face from your servant;
answer quickly for I am in distress.
Come close to my soul and redeem me;
ransom me pressed by my foes.

You know how they taunt and deride me;
my oppressors are all before you.
Taunts have broken my heart;
I have reached the end of my strength.
I looked in vain for compassion,
for consolers; not one could I find.

For food they gave me poison;
in my thirst they gave me vinegar to drink.

I will praise God's name with a song;
I will glorify him with thanksgiving.
A gift pleasing God more than oxen,
more than beasts prepared for sacrifice.

The poor when they see it will be glad,
and God-seeking hearts will revive;
for the Lord listens to the needy
and does not spurn his servants in their chains.
Let the heavens and the earth give him praise,
the sea and all its living creatures.

For God will bring help to Sion,
and rebuild the cities of Judah:
and men shall dwell there in possession.
The sons of his servants shall inherit it;
those who love his name shall dwell there.

69 (70)

O God, make haste to my rescue;
Lord, come to my aid!

Let there be rejoicing and gladness
for all who seek you.
Let them say for ever: 'God is great',
who love your saving help.

As for me, wretched and poor,
come to me, O God.
You are my rescuer, my help,
O Lord, do not delay.

70 (71)

In you, O Lord, I take refuge:
let me never be put to shame.
In your justice rescue me, free me:
pay heed to me and save me.

Be a rock where I can take refuge,
a mighty stronghold to save me;
for you are my rock, my stronghold.

It is you, O Lord, who are my hope:
my trust, O Lord, since my youth.
On you I have leaned from my birth,
from my mother's womb you have been my help.
My hope has always been in you.

My fate has filled many with awe
but you are my strong refuge.
My lips are filled with your praise,
with your glory all the day long.
Do not reject me now that I am old;
when my strength fails do not forsake me.

O God, do not stay far off:
my God, make haste to help me!

As for me, I will always hope and praise you more and
more.

My lips will tell of your justice
and day by day of your help
(though I can never tell it all).

I will declare the Lord's mighty deeds:
proclaiming your justice, yours alone.
O God, you have taught me from my youth,
and I proclaim your wonders still.

Now that I am old and grey-headed,
do not forsake me, God.
Let me tell of your power to all ages,
praise your strength and justice to the skies,
tell of you who have worked such wonders.
O God, who is like you?

You have burdened me with bitter troubles
but you will give me back my life.
You will raise me from the depths of the earth;
you will exalt me and console me again.

So I will give you thanks on the lyre
for your faithful love, my God.
To you will I sing with the harp;
to you, the Holy One of Israel.
When I sing to you my lips shall rejoice
and my soul, which you have redeemed.

And all day long my tongue
shall tell the tale of your justice.

71 (72)

O God, give your judgment to the king,
to a king's son your justice,
that he may judge your people in justice
and your poor in right judgment.

May the mountains bring forth peace for the people,
and the hills, justice.
May he defend the poor of the people
and save the children of the needy.

He shall endure like the sun and the moon
from age to age.
He shall descend like rain on the meadow,
like raindrops on the earth.

In his days justice shall flourish
and peace till the moon fails.
He shall rule from sea to sea,
from the Great River to the earth's bounds.

For he shall save the poor when they cry,
and the needy who are helpless.
He will have pity on the weak
and save the lives of the poor.

From oppression he will rescue their lives,
to him their blood is dear.

(Long may he live,
may the gold of Sheba be given him.)
They shall pray for him without ceasing
and bless him all the day.

May corn be abundant in the land
to the peaks of the mountains.
May its fruit rustle like Lebanon;
may men flourish in the cities
like grass on the earth.

May his name be blessed for ever
and endure like the sun.
Every tribe shall be blessed in him,
all nations bless his name.

Blessed be the Lord, God of Israel,
Who alone works wonders,
ever blessed his glorious name.
Let his glory fill the earth.
Amen! Amen!

72 (73)

How good God is to Israel,
to those who are pure of heart.
Yet my feet came close to stumbling,
my steps had almost slipped.

How useless to keep my heart pure
and wash my hands in innocence,
when I was stricken all day long,
suffered punishment day after day.
Then I said: 'If I should speak like that,
I should betray the race of your sons.'

I strove to fathom this problem,
too hard for my mind to understand.

And so when my heart grew embittered
and when I was cut to the quick,
I was stupid and did not understand,
no better than a beast in your sight.

Yet I was always in your presence;
you were holding me by my right hand.
You will guide me by your counsel
and so you will lead me to glory.

What else have I in heaven but you?
Apart from you I want nothing on earth.
My body and my heart faint for joy;
God is my possession for ever.

To be near God is my happiness.
I have made the Lord God my refuge.
I will tell of all your works
at the gates of the city of Sion.

73 (74)

O God, remember your people whom you chose long
    ago,
the tribe you redeemed to be your own possession,
the mountain of Sion where you made your dwelling.

God is our king from time past,
the giver of help through all the land.
It was you who divided the sea by your might,
who shattered the heads of the monsters in the sea.

It was you who crushed Leviathan's heads
and gave him as food to the untamed beasts.
It was you who opened springs and torrents;
it was you who dried up ever-flowing rivers.

Yours is the day and yours is the night.
It was you who appointed the light and the sun:
it was you who fixed the bounds of the earth:
you who made both summer and winter.

74 (75)

We give thanks to you, O God,
we give thanks and call upon your name.
We recount your wonderful deeds.

'When I reach the appointed time,
then I will judge with justice.
Though the earth and all who dwell in it may rock,
it is I who uphold its pillars.'

For neither from the east nor from the west,
nor from desert or mountains comes judgment,
but God himself is the judge.
One he humbles, another he exalts.

As for me, I will rejoice for ever
and sing psalms to Jacob's God.

76 (77)

I cry aloud to God,
cry aloud to God that he may hear me.

In the day of my distress I sought the Lord.
At night my hands were raised without ceasing;
my soul refused to be consoled.
I remembered my God and I groaned.
I pondered and my spirit fainted.

You withheld sleep from my eyes.
I was troubled, I could not speak.
I thought of the days of long ago
and remembered the years long past.
At night I mused within my heart.
I pondered and my spirit questioned.

'Will the Lord reject us for ever?
Will he show us his favour no more?
Has his love vanished for ever?
Has his promise come to an end?
Does God forget his mercy,
or in anger withhold his compassion?'

I said: 'This is what causes my grief;
that the way of the Most High has changed.'
I remember the deeds of the Lord,
I remember your wonders of old,

I muse on all your works
and ponder your mighty deeds.

Your ways, O God, are holy.
What god is great as our God?
You are the God who works wonders.
You showed your power among the peoples,
your strong arm redeemed your people,
the sons of Jacob and Joseph.

The waters saw you, O God,
the waters saw you and trembled;
the depths were moved with terror.
The clouds poured down rain,
the skies sent forth their voice;
your arrows flashed to and fro.

Your thunder rolled round the sky,
your flashes lit up the world.
The earth was moved and trembled
when your way led through the sea,
your path through the mighty waters
and no one saw your footprints.

You guided your people like a flock
by the hand of Moses and Aaron.

77 (78)

Give heed, my people, to my teaching;
turn your ear to the words of my mouth.
I will open my mouth in a parable
and reveal hidden lessons of the past.

The things we have heard and understood,
the things our fathers have told us
we will not hide from their children
but will tell them to the next generation:

the glories of the Lord and his might
and the marvellous deeds he has done,
the witness he gave to Jacob,
the law he established in Israel.

He gave a command to our fathers
to make it known to their children
that the next generation might know it,
the children yet to be born.

They too should arise and tell their sons
that they too should set their hope in God
and never forget God's deeds,
but keep every one of his commands:

so that they might not be like their fathers,
a defiant and rebellious race,

a race whose heart was fickle,
whose spirit was unfaithful to God.

✳

The sons of Ephraim, armed with the bow,
turned back in the day of battle.
They failed to keep God's covenant
and would not walk according to his law.

They forgot the things he had done,
the marvellous deeds he had shown them.
He did wonders in the sight of their fathers,
in Egypt, in the plains of Zoan.

He divided the sea and led them through
and made the waters stand up like a wall.
By day he led them with a cloud:
By night, with a light of fire.

He split the rocks in the desert.
He gave them plentiful drink as from the deep.
He made streams flow out from the rock
and made waters run down like rivers.

✳

Yet still they sinned against him;
they defied the Most High in the desert.
In their heart they put God to the test
by demanding the food they craved.

They even spoke against God.
They said: 'Is it possible for God
to prepare a table in the desert?'

It was he who struck the rock,
water flowed and swept down in torrents.
But can he also give us bread?
Can he provide meat for his people?

Yet he commanded the clouds above
and opened the gates of heaven.
He rained down manna for their food,
and gave them bread from heaven.

Mere men ate the bread of angels.
He sent them abundance of food:
he made the east wind blow from heaven
and roused the south wind by his might.

He rained food on them like dust,
winged fowl like the sands of the sea.
He let it fall in the midst of their camp
and all around their tents.

So they ate and had their fill;
for he gave them all they craved.

When he slew them then they would seek him,
return and seek him in earnest.
They would remember that God was their rock,
God the Most High their redeemer.

But the words they spoke were mere flattery;
they lied to him with their lips.
For their hearts were not truly with him;
they were not faithful to his covenant.

Yet he who is full of compassion
forgave their sin and spared them.

79 (80)

O Shepherd of Israel, hear us,
you who lead Joseph's flock,
shine forth from your cherubim throne
upon Ephraim, Benjamin, Manasse.
O Lord, rouse up your might,
O Lord, come to our help.

God of hosts, bring us back;
let your face shine on us and we shall be saved.

Lord God of hosts, how long
will you frown on your people's plea?
You have fed them with tears for their bread,
and abundance of tears for their drink.
You have made us the taunt of our neighbours,
our enemies laugh us to scorn.

God of hosts, bring us back;
let your face shine on us and we shall be saved.

You brought a vine out of Egypt;
before it you cleared the ground;
it took root and spread through the land.

The mountains were covered with its shadow,
the cedars of God with its boughs.
It stretched out its branches to the sea,
to the Great River it stretched out its shoots.

Then why have you broken down its walls?
It is plucked by all who pass by.
It is ravaged by the boar of the forest,
devoured by the beasts of the field.

God of hosts, turn again, we implore,
look down from heaven and see.
Visit this vine and protect it,
the vine your right hand has planted.

May your hand be on the man you have chosen,
the man you have given your strength.
And we shall never forsake you again:
give us life that we may call upon your name.

God of hosts, bring us back;
let your face shine on us and we shall be saved.

80 (81)

Ring out your joy to God our strength,
shout in triumph to the God of Jacob.

Raise a song and sound the timbrel,
the sweet-sounding harp and the lute,
blow the trumpet at the new moon,
when the moon is full, on our feast.

For this is Israel's law,
a command of the God of Jacob.
He imposed it as a rule on Joseph,
When he went out against the land of Egypt.

A voice I did not know said to me:
'I freed your shoulder from the burden;
your hands were freed from the load.
You called in distress and I saved you.

'I answered, concealed in the storm cloud:
at the waters of Meribah I tested you.
Listen, my people, to my warning,
O Israel, if only you would heed!

'I am the Lord your God,
Who brought you from the land of Egypt.
Open wide your mouth and I will fill it.

'But my people did not heed my voice
and Israel would not obey,
so I left them in their stubbornness of heart
to follow their own designs.

'O that my people would heed me,
that Israel would walk in my ways!'

81 (82)

God stands in the divine assembly.
In the midst of the gods he gives judgment.

Do justice for the weak and the orphan,
defend the afflicted and the needy.
Rescue the weak and the poor;
set them free from the hand of the wicked.

Unperceiving, they grope in the darkness
and the order of the world is shaken.
I have said to you: 'You are gods
and all of you, sons of the Most High.'
And yet, 'You shall die like men,
you shall fall like any of the princes.'

Arise O God, judge the earth,
for you rule all the nations.

83 (84)

How lovely is your dwelling place,
Lord, God of hosts.

My soul is longing and yearning,
is yearning for the courts of the Lord.
My heart and my soul ring out their joy
to God, the living God.

The sparrow herself finds a home
and the swallow a nest for her brood;
she lays her young by your altars,
Lord of hosts, my king and my God.

They are happy, who dwell in your house,
for ever singing your praise.
They are happy, whose strength is in you,
in whose hearts are the roads to Sion.

As they go through the Bitter Valley
they make it a place of springs,
the autumn rain covers it with blessings.
They walk with ever growing strength,
they will see the God of gods in Sion.

O Lord God of hosts, hear my prayer,
give ear, O God of Jacob.
Turn your eyes, O God, our shield,
look on the face of your anointed.

One day within your courts
is better than a thousand elsewhere.

For the Lord God is a rampart, a shield;
he will give us his favour and glory.
The Lord will not refuse any good
to those who walk without blame.

Lord, God of hosts,
happy the man who trusts in you!

84 (85)

O Lord, you once favoured your land
and revived the fortunes of Jacob,
you forgave the guilt of your people
and covered all their sins.

Will you not restore again our life
that your people may rejoice in you?
Let us see, O Lord, your mercy
and give us your saving help.

*

I will hear what the Lord God has to say,
a voice that speaks of peace,
peace for his people and his friends
and those who turn to him in their hearts.
His help is near for those who fear him
and his glory will dwell in our land.

Mercy and faithfulness have met;
justice and peace have embraced.
Faithfulness shall spring from the earth
and justice look down from heaven.

The Lord will make us prosper
and our earth shall yield its fruit.
Justice shall march before him
and peace shall follow his steps.

85 (86)

Turn your ear, O Lord, and give answer
for I am poor and needy.
Preserve my life, for I am faithful:
save the servant who trusts in you.

You are my God, have mercy on me, Lord,
for I cry to you all the day long.
Give joy to your servant, O Lord,
for to you I lift up my soul.

O Lord, you are good and forgiving,
full of love to all who call.
Give heed, O Lord, to my prayer
and attend to the sound of my voice.

In the day of distress I will call
and surely you will reply.
Among the gods there is none like you, O Lord;
nor work to compare with yours.

All the nations shall come to adore you
and glorify your name, O Lord:
for you are great and do marvellous deeds,
you who alone are God.

Show me, Lord, your way
so that I may walk in your truth.
Guide my heart to fear your name.

I will praise you, Lord my God, with all my heart
and glorify your name for ever;
for your love to me has been great:
you have saved me from the depths of the grave.

But you, God of mercy and compassion,
abounding in love and truth,
turn and take pity on me.

O give your strength to your servant
and save your handmaid's son.
Show me a sign of your favour.

86 (87)

On the holy mountain is his city
cherished by the Lord.
The Lord prefers the gates of Sion
to all Jacob's dwellings.
Of you are told glorious things,
O city of God!

Babylon and Egypt I will count
among those who know me;
Philistia, Tyre, Ethiopia,
these will be her children
and Sion shall be called 'Mother'
for all shall be her children.

It is he, the Lord Most High,
who gives each his place.
In his register of peoples he writes:
'These are her children.'
And while they dance they will sing:
'In you all find their home.'

88 (89)

I will sing for ever of your love, O Lord;
through all ages my mouth will proclaim your truth.
Of this I am sure, that your love lasts for ever,
that your truth is firmly established as the heavens.

'I have made a covenant with my chosen one;
I have sworn to David my servant:
I will establish your dynasty for ever
and set up your throne through all ages.'

The heavens proclaim your wonders, O Lord;
the assembly of your holy ones proclaim your truth.
For who in the skies can compare with the Lord
or who is like the Lord among the sons of God?

O Lord God of hosts, who is your equal?
You are mighty, O Lord, and truth is your garment.

It is you who rule the sea in its pride;
it is you who still the surging of its waves.

The heavens are yours, the world is yours.
It is you who founded the earth and all it holds;
it is you who created the North and the South.
Tabor and Hermon shout with joy at your name.

Yours is a mighty arm, O Lord;
Your hand is strong, your right hand ready.
Justice and right are the pillars of your throne,
love and truth walk in your presence.

Happy the people who acclaim such a king,
who walk, O Lord, in the light of your face,
who find their joy every day in your name,
who make your justice the source of their bliss.

For it is you, O Lord, who are the glory of their strength;
it is by your favour that our might is exalted:
for our ruler is in the keeping of the Lord;
our king in the keeping of the Holy One of Israel.

Of old you spoke in a vision.
To your friends the prophets you said:
'I have set the crown on a warrior,
I have exalted one chosen from the people.

'I have found David my servant
and with my holy oil anointed him.
My hand shall always be with him
and my arm shall make him strong.

'My truth and my love shall be with him;
by my name his might shall be exalted.
I will stretch out his hand to the sea
and his right hand as far as the River.

'He will say to me: "You are my father,
my God, the rock who saves me."
And I will make him my first-born,
the highest of the kings of the earth.

'I will keep my love for him always;
for him my covenant shall endure;
I will establish his dynasty for ever,
make his throne as lasting as the heavens.

'I will never take back my love:
my truth will never fail.

'I will never violate my covenant
nor go back on the word I have spoken.
Once for all, I have sworn by my holiness.
I will never lie to David.

'His dynasty shall last for ever.
In my sight his throne is like the sun;
like the moon, it shall endure for ever,
a faithful witness in the skies.'

Blessed be the Lord for ever. Amen, amen!

89 (90)

O Lord, you have been our refuge
from one generation to the next.
Before the mountains were born
or the earth or the world brought forth,
you are God, without beginning or end.

You turn men back into dust
and say: 'Go back, sons of men.'
To your eyes a thousand years are like yesterday, come
    and gone,
no more than a watch in the night.

You sweep men away like a dream,
like grass which springs up in the morning.
In the morning it springs up and flowers:
by evening it withers and fades.

Our guilt lies open before you;
our secrets in the light of your face.

Our life is over like a sigh.
Our span is seventy years
or eighty for those who are strong.

And most of these are emptiness and pain.
They pass swiftly and we are gone.

Make us know the shortness of our life
that we may gain wisdom of heart.
Show pity to your servants.

In the morning, fill us with your love;
we shall exult and rejoice all our days.
Give us joy to balance our affliction
for the years when we knew misfortune.

Show forth your work to your servants;
let your glory shine on their children.
Let the favour of the Lord be upon us:
Give success to the work of our hands.
(Give success to the work of our hands.)

90 (91)

He who dwells in the shelter of the Most High
and abides in the shade of the Almighty
says to the Lord: 'My refuge,
my stronghold, my God in whom I trust!'

It is he who will free you from the snare
of the fowler who seeks to destroy you;
he will conceal you with his pinions
and under his wings you will find refuge.

You will not fear the terror of the night,
nor the arrow that flies by day,
nor the plague that prowls in the darkness,
nor the scourge that lays waste at noon.

A thousand may fall at your side,
ten thousand fall at your right,
you, it will never approach;
his faithfulness is buckler and shield.

You who have said: 'Lord, my refuge!'
and have made the Most High your dwelling.

Upon you no evil shall fall,
no plague approach where you dwell.
For you has he commanded his angels,
to keep you in all your ways.

They shall bear you upon their hands
lest you strike your foot against a stone.
On the lion and the viper you will tread;
you will trample the young lion and the dragon.

His love he set on me, so I will rescue him;
protect him for he knows my name.
When he calls I shall answer: 'I am with you.'
I will save him in distress and give him glory.

With length of life I will content him;
I shall let him see my saving power.

91 (92)

It is good to give thanks to the Lord,
to make music to your name, O Most High,
to proclaim your love in the morning
and your truth in the watches of the night,
on the ten-stringed lyre and the lute,
with the murmuring sound of the harp.

Your deeds, O Lord, have made me glad;
for the work of your hands I shout with joy.
O Lord, how great are your works!
How deep are your designs!

The just will flourish like the palm-tree
and grow like a Lebanon cedar.

Planted in the house of the Lord
They will flourish in the courts of our God,
still bearing fruit when they are old,
still full of sap, still green,
to proclaim that the Lord is just,
in him, my rock, there is no wrong.

92 (93)

The Lord is king, with majesty enrobed;
the Lord has robed himself with might,
he has girded himself with power.

The world you made firm, not to be moved;
your throne has stood firm from of old.
From all eternity, O Lord, you are.

The waters have lifted up, O Lord,
the waters have lifted up their voice,
the waters have lifted up their thunder.

Greater than the roar of mighty waters,
more glorious than the surging of the sea,
the Lord is glorious on high.

Truly your decrees are to be trusted.
Holiness is fitting to your house,
O Lord, until the end of time.

94 (95)

Come ring out our joy to the Lord;
hail the rock who saves us.
Let us come before him, giving thanks,
with songs let us hail the Lord.

A mighty God is the Lord,
a great king above all gods.
In his hand are the depths of earth;
the heights of the mountains are his.
To him belongs the sea, for he made it;
and the dry land shaped by his hands.

Come in; let us bow and bend low;
let us kneel before the God who made us,
for he is our God and we
the people who belongs to his pasture,
the flock that is led by his hand.

O that today you would listen to his voice!
'Harden not your hearts as at Meribah,
as on that day at Massah in the desert
when your fathers put me to the test;
when they tried me, though they saw my work.'

95 (96)

O sing a new song to the Lord,
sing to the Lord all the earth.
O sing to the Lord, bless his name.

Proclaim his help day by day,
tell among the nations his glory,
and his wonders among all the peoples.

The Lord is great and worthy of praise,
to be feared above all gods;

It was the Lord who made the heavens,
his are majesty and state and power
and splendour in his holy place.

Give the Lord, you families of peoples,
give the Lord glory and power,
give the Lord the glory of his name.

Bring an offering and enter his courts,
worship the Lord in his temple.
O earth, tremble before him.

Proclaim to the nations: 'God is king.'
The world he made firm in its place;
he will judge the peoples in fairness.

Let the heavens rejoice and earth be glad.
Let the sea and all within it thunder praise,
let the land and all it bears rejoice,
all the trees of the wood shout for joy

At the presence of the Lord: for he comes,
he comes to rule the earth.
With justice he will rule the world,
he will judge the peoples with his truth.

96 (97)

The Lord is king, let earth rejoice,
the many coastlands be glad.
Cloud and darkness are his raiment;
his throne, justice and right.

His lightnings light up the world,
the earth trembles at the sight.

The mountains melt like wax
before the Lord of all the earth.
The skies proclaim his justice;
all peoples see his glory.

All you spirits, worship him.

Sion hears and is glad;
the people of Judah rejoice
because of your judgments, O Lord.

For you indeed are the Lord:
most high above all the earth,
exalted far above all spirits.

He guards the souls of his saints.
Light shines forth for the just
and joy for the upright of heart.
Rejoice, you just, in the Lord;
give glory to his holy name.

97 (98)

Sing a new song to the Lord;
for he has worked wonders.
His right hand and his holy arm
have brought salvation.

The Lord has made known his salvation;
has shown his justice to the nations.
He has remembered his truth and love
for the house of Israel.

All the ends of the earth have seen
the salvation of our God.
Shout to the Lord all the earth,
ring out your joy.

Sing psalms to the Lord with the harp,
with the sound of music.
With trumpets and the sound of the horn
acclaim the King, the Lord.

Let the sea and all within it, thunder;
the world, and all its peoples.
Let the rivers clap their hands
and the hills ring out their joy

At the presence of the Lord: for he comes,
he comes to rule the earth.
He will rule the world with justice
and the peoples with fairness.

98 (99)

The Lord is King; the peoples tremble.
He is throned amid the cherubim; earth quakes.
The Lord is great in Sion.

He is supreme over all the peoples.
Let them praise his name, so terrible and great.
He is holy, full of power.

You are a king who loves what is right;
you have established equity, justice and right;
you have established them in Jacob.

Exalt the Lord our God;
bow down before Sion, his footstool.
He the Lord is holy.

Among his priests were Aaron and Moses,
among those who invoked his name was Samuel.
They invoked the Lord and he answered.

To them he spoke in the pillar of cloud.
They did his will; they kept the law,
which he, the Lord, had given.

O Lord our God, you answered them.
For them you were a God who forgives.

Exalt the Lord our God;
bow down before his holy mountain
for the Lord our God is holy.

99 (100)

Cry out with joy to the Lord, all the earth.
Serve the Lord with gladness.
Come before him, singing for joy.

Know that he, the Lord, is God.
He made us, we belong to him,
we are his people, the sheep of his flock.

Go within his gates, giving thanks.
Enter his courts with songs of praise.
Give thanks to him and bless his name.

Indeed, how good is the Lord,
eternal his merciful love.
He is faithful from age to age.

101 (102)

O Lord, listen to my prayer
and let my cry for help reach you.
Do not hide your face from me
in the day of my distress.
Turn your ear towards me
and answer me quickly when I call.

For my days are vanishing like smoke,
my bones burn away like a fire.
My heart is withered like the grass.
I forget to eat my bread.
I cry with all my strength
and my skin clings to my bones.

I have become like a pelican in the wilderness,
like an owl in desolate places.
I lie awake and I moan
like some lonely bird on a roof.

The bread I eat is ashes;
my drink is mingled with tears.
My days are like a passing shadow
and I wither away like the grass.

But you, O Lord, will endure for ever
and your name from age to age.
You will arise and have mercy on Sion:

for this is the time to have mercy,
(yes, the time appointed has come)
for your servants love her very stones,
are moved with pity even for her dust.

The nations shall fear the name of the Lord
and all the earth's kings your glory,
when the Lord shall build up Sion again
and appear in all his glory.
Then he will turn to the prayers of the helpless;
he will not despise their prayers.

Let this be written for ages to come
that a people yet unborn may praise the Lord;
for the Lord leaned down from his sanctuary on high.
He looked down from heaven to the earth
that he might hear the groans of the prisoners
and free those condemned to die.

The sons of your servants shall dwell untroubled
and their race shall endure before you
that the name of the Lord may be proclaimed in Sion
and his praise in the heart of Jerusalem,
when peoples and kingdoms are gathered together
to pay their homage to the Lord.

*

He has broken my strength in mid-course;
he has shortened the days of my life.
I say to God: 'Do not take me away
before my days are completed,
you, whose days last from age to age.

'Long ago you founded the earth
and the heavens are the work of your hands.
They will perish but you will remain.
They will all wear out like a garment.
You will change them like clothes that are changed.
But you neither change, nor have an end.'

102 (103)

My soul, give thanks to the Lord,
all my being, bless his holy name.
My soul, give thanks to the Lord
and never forget all his blessings.

It is he who forgives all your guilt,
who heals every one of your ills,
who redeems your life from the grave,
who crowns you with love and compassion,
who fills your life with good things,
renewing your youth like an eagle's.

The Lord does deeds of justice,
gives judgment for all who are oppressed.
He made known his ways to Moses
and his deeds to Israel's sons.

The Lord is compassion and love,
slow to anger and rich in mercy.
He does not treat us according to our sins
nor repay us according to our faults.

For as the heavens are high above the earth,
so strong is his love for those who fear him.
As far as the east is from the west,
so far does he remove our sins.

As a father has compassion on his sons,
the Lord has pity on those who fear him;
for he knows of what we are made,
he remembers that we are dust.

As for man, his days are like grass;
he flowers like the flower of the field;
the wind blows, and he is gone,
and his place never sees him again.

But the love of the Lord is everlasting
upon those who hold him in fear;
his justice reaches out to children's children
when they keep his covenant in truth,
when they keep his will in their mind.

The Lord has set his sway in heaven
and his kingdom is ruling over all.
Give thanks to the Lord, all his angels,
mighty in power, fulfilling his word,
who heed the voice of his word.

Give thanks to the Lord, all his hosts,
his servants who do his will.
Give thanks to the Lord, all his works,
in every place where he rules.
My soul, give thanks to the Lord!

103A (104A)

Bless the Lord, my soul!
Lord God, how great you are,
clothed in majesty and glory,
wrapped in light as in a robe!

You stretch out the heavens like a tent.
Above the rains you build your dwelling.
You make the clouds your chariot,
you walk on the wings of the wind,
you make the winds your messengers
and flashing fire your servants.

You founded the earth on its base,
to stand firm from age to age.
You wrapped it with the ocean like a cloak:
the waters stood higher than the mountains.

At your threat they took to flight;
at the voice of your thunder they fled.
They rose over the mountains and flowed down
to the place which you had appointed.
You set limits they might not pass
lest they return to cover the earth.

You make springs gush forth in the valleys;
they flow in between the hills.
They give drink to all the beasts of the field;
the wild asses quench their thirst.
On their banks dwell the birds of heaven;
from the branches they sing their song.

From your dwelling you water the hills;
earth drinks its fill of your gift.
You make the grass grow for the cattle;
and the plants to serve man's needs,
that he may bring forth bread from the earth
and wine, to cheer man's heart;
oil to make his face shine,
and bread to strengthen man's heart.

The trees of the Lord drink their fill,
the cedars he planted on Lebanon;
there the birds build their nests:
on the tree-top the stork has her home.
The goats find a home on the mountains
and rabbits hide in the rocks.

You made the moon to mark the months;
the sun knows the time for its setting.
When you spread the darkness it is night
and all the beasts of the forest creep forth.
The young lions roar for their prey
and ask their food from God.

At the rising of the sun they steal away
and go to rest in their dens.
Man goes forth to his work,
to labour till evening falls.

103B (104B)

How many are your works, O Lord!
In wisdom you have made them all.
The earth is full of your riches.

There is the sea, vast and wide,
with its moving swarms past counting,
living things great and small.
The ships are moving there
and the monsters you made to play with.

All of these look to you
to give them their food in due season.
You give it, they gather it up:
you open your hand, they have their fill.

You hide your face, they are dismayed;
you take back your spirit, they die,
returning to the dust from which they come.
You send forth your spirit, they are created;
and you renew the face of the earth.

May the glory of the Lord last for ever!
May the Lord rejoice in his works!
He looks on the earth and it trembles;
the mountains send forth smoke at his touch.

I will sing to the Lord all my life,
make music to my God while I live.
May my thoughts be pleasing to him.
I find my joy in the Lord.

Bless the Lord, my soul.

104 (105)

Alleluia!

Give thanks to the Lord, tell his name;
make known his deeds among the peoples.

O sing to him, sing his praise;
tell all his wonderful works!
Be proud of his holy name;
let the hearts that seek the Lord rejoice.

Consider the Lord and his strength;
constantly seek his face.
Remember the wonders he has done,
his miracles, the judgments he spoke.

O children of Abraham, his servant,
O sons of the Jacob he chose.
He the Lord, is our God:
his judgments prevail in all the earth.

He remembers his covenant for ever,
his promise for a thousand generations,
the covenant he made with Abraham,
the oath he swore to Isaac.

He confirmed it for Jacob as a law,
for Israel as a covenant for ever.
He said: 'I am giving you a land,
Canaan, your appointed heritage.'

When they were few in number,
a handful of strangers in the land,
when they wandered from country to country
and from one kingdom to another,

He allowed no one to oppress them;
he admonished kings on their account;
'Do not touch my anointed;
do no harm to any of my prophets.'

But he called down a famine on the land;
he broke the staff that supported them.
He had sent a man before them,
Joseph, sold as a slave.

His feet were put in chains,
his neck was bound with iron,
until what he said came to pass
and the Lord's word proved him true.

Then the king sent and released him;
the ruler of the peoples set him free,
making him master of his house
and ruler of all he possessed,

To instruct his princes as he pleased
and to teach his elders wisdom.
So Israel came into Egypt,
Jacob lived in the country of Ham.

Egypt rejoiced when they left,
for dread had fallen upon them.
He spread a cloud as a screen
and fire to give light in the darkness.

When they asked for food he sent quails;
he filled them with bread from heaven.
He pierced the rock to give them water;
it gushed forth in the desert like a river.

For he remembered his holy word,
which he gave to Abraham his servant.
So he brought out his people with joy,
His chosen ones with shouts of rejoicing.

And he gave them the land of the nations.
They took the fruit of other men's toil,
that thus they might keep his precepts,
that thus they might observe his laws.

Alleluia!

105 (106)

Alleluia!

O give thanks to the Lord for he is good;
for his great love is without end.
Who can tell the Lord's mighty deeds?
Who can recount all his praise?

They are happy who do what is right,
who at all times do what is just.
O Lord, remember me
out of the love you have for your people.

Come to me, Lord, with your help
that I may see the joy of your chosen ones
and may rejoice in the gladness of your nation
and share the glory of your people.

Our sin is the sin of our fathers;
we have done wrong, our deeds have been evil.
Our fathers when they were in Egypt
paid no heed to your wonderful deeds.

They forgot the greatness of your love;
at the Red Sea defied the Most High.
Yet he saved them for the sake of his name,
in order to make known his power.

106 (107)

'O give thanks to the Lord for he is good;
for his great love is without end.'

Let them say this, the Lord's redeemed,
whom he redeemed from the hand of the foe
and gathered from far-off lands,
from east and west, north and south.

❋

Some wandered in the desert, in the wilderness,
finding no way to a city they could dwell in.
Hungry they were and thirsty;
their soul was fainting within them.

Then they cried to the Lord in their need
and he rescued them from their distress
and he led them along the right way,
to reach a city they could dwell in.

Let them thank the Lord for his love,
for the wonders he does for men.
For he satisfies the thirsty soul;
he fills the hungry with good things.

Some were sick on account of their sins
and afflicted on account of their guilt.
They had a loathing for every food;
they came close to the gates of death.

Then they cried to the Lord in their need
and he rescued them from their distress.
He sent forth his word to heal them
and saved their life from the grave.

Let them thank the Lord for his love,
for the wonders he does for men.
Let them offer a sacrifice of thanks
and tell of his deeds with rejoicing.

Some sailed to the sea in ships
to trade on the mighty waters.
These men have seen the Lord's deeds,
the wonders he does in the deep.

For he spoke; he summoned the gale,
tossing the waves of the sea
up to heaven and back into the deep;
their soul melted away in their distress.

They staggered, reeled like drunken men,
for all their skill was gone.
Then they cried to the Lord in their need
and he rescued them from their distress.

He stilled the storm to a whisper:
all the waves of the sea were hushed;
They rejoiced because of the calm
and he led them to the haven they desired.

Let them thank the Lord for his love,
the wonders he does for men.
Let them exalt him in the gathering of the people
and praise him in the meeting of the elders.

He changes streams into a desert,
springs of water into thirsty ground,
a fruitful land into a salt waste.

But he changes desert into streams,
thirsty ground into springs of water.
There he settles the hungry
and they built a city to dwell in.

They sow fields and plant their vines;
these yield crops for the harvest.
He blesses them; they grow in numbers.
He does not let their herds decrease.

But he raises the needy from distress;
makes families numerous as a flock.
The upright see it and rejoice
but all who do wrong are silenced.

Whoever is wise, let him heed these things
and consider the love of the Lord.

103

107 (108)

My heart is ready, O God;
I will sing, sing your praise.
Awake, my soul;
awake, lyre and harp.
I will awake the dawn.

I will thank you, Lord, among the peoples,
praise you among the nations;
for your love reaches to the heavens
and your truth to the skies.
O God, arise above the heavens;
may your glory shine on earth!

O come and deliver your friends,
help with your right hand and reply.

109 (110)

The Lord's revelation to my Master:
'Sit on my right:

'A prince from the day of your birth
on the holy mountains:
from the womb before the daybreak I begot you.'

The Lord has sworn an oath he will not change.
'You are a priest for ever,
a priest like Melchizedeck of old.'

110 (111)

Alleluia!

I will thank the Lord with all my heart
in the meeting of the just and their assembly.
Great are the works of the Lord;
to be pondered by all who love them.

Majestic and glorious his work,
his justice stands firm for ever.
He makes us remember his wonders.
The Lord is compassion and love.

He gives food to those who fear him;
keeps his covenant ever in mind.

His works are justice and truth:
his precepts are all of them sure,
standing firm for ever and ever:
they are made in uprightness and truth.

He has sent deliverance to his people
and established his covenant for ever.
Holy his name, to be feared.

To fear the Lord is the beginning of wisdom;
all who do so prove themselves wise.
His praise shall last for ever!

111 (112)

Alleluia!

Happy the man who fears the Lord,
who takes delight in his commands.
His sons will be powerful on earth;
the children of the upright are blessed.

Riches and wealth are in his house;
his justice stands firm for ever.
He is a light in the darkness for the upright:
he is generous, merciful and just.

The good man takes pity and lends,
he conducts his affairs with honour.
The just man will never waver:
he will be remembered for ever.

He has no fear of evil news;
with a firm heart he trusts in the Lord.
With a steadfast heart he will not fear;

Open-handed, he gives to the poor;
his justice stands firm for ever.
His head will be raised in glory.

112 (113)

Alleluia!

Praise, O servants of the Lord,
praise the name of the Lord!
May the name of the Lord be blessed
both now and for evermore!
From the rising of the sun to its setting
praised be the name of the Lord!

High above all nations is the Lord,
above the heavens his glory.
Who is like the Lord, our God,
Who has risen on high to his throne
yet stoops from the heights to look down,
to look down upon heaven and earth?

From the dust he lifts up the lowly,
from the dungheap he raises the poor
to set him in the company of princes,
yes, with the princes of his people.
To the childless wife he gives a home
and gladdens her heart with children.

113 (114)

Alleluia!

When Israel came forth from Egypt,
Jacob's sons from an alien people,
Judah became the Lord's temple,
Israel became his kingdom.

The sea fled at the sight:
the Jordan turned back on its course,
the mountains leapt like rams
and the hills like yearling sheep.

Why was it, sea, that you fled,
that you turned back, Jordan, on your course?
Mountains, that you leapt like rams,
hills, like yearling sheep?

Tremble, O earth, before the Lord,
in the presence of the God of Jacob,
who turns the rock into a pool
and flint into a spring of water.

Sons of Israel, trust in the Lord;
he is their help and their shield.
Sons of Aaron, trust in the Lord;
he is their help and their shield.

You who fear him, trust in the Lord;
he is their help and their shield.
He remembers us, will give us his blessing;
he will bless the sons of Israel.
He will bless the sons of Aaron.

The Lord will bless those who fear him,
the little no less than the great:
to you may the Lord grant increase,
to you and all your children.

May you be blessed by the Lord,
the maker of heaven and earth.
The heavens belong to the Lord
but the earth he has given to men.

We who live, bless the Lord
now and for ever, Amen.

114 (116A)

Alleluia!

I love the Lord for he has heard
the cry of my appeal;
for he turned his ear to me
in the day when I called him.

They surrounded me, the snares of death,
with the anguish of the tomb;
they caught me, sorrow and distress.
I called on the Lord's name.

O Lord my God, deliver me!

How gracious is the Lord, and just;
our God has compassion.
The Lord protects the simple hearts;
I was helpless so he saved me.

Turn back, my soul, to your rest:
for the Lord has been good;
he has kept my soul from death,
(my eyes from tears)
and my feet from stumbling.

I will walk in the presence of the Lord
in the land of the living.

115 & 116 (116B & 117)

I trusted, even when I said:
'I am sorely afflicted,'
and when I said in my alarm:
'No man can be trusted.'

How can I repay the Lord
for his goodness to me?
The cup of salvation I will raise;
I will call on the Lord's name.

My vows to the Lord I will fulfil
before all his people.
O precious in the eyes of the Lord
is the death of his faithful.

Your servant, Lord, your servant am I;
you have loosened my bonds.
A thanksgiving sacrifice I make:
I will call on the Lord's name.

My vows to the Lord I will fulfil
before all his people,
in the courts of the house of the Lord,
in your midst, O Jerusalem.

Alleluia!

O praise the Lord, all you nations,
Acclaim him all you peoples!

Strong is his love for us;
he is faithful for ever.

117 (118)

Alleluia!

Give thanks to the Lord for he is good,
for his love has no end.

Let the sons of Israel say:
'His love has no end.'
Let the sons of Aaron say:
'His love has no end.'
Let those who fear the Lord say:
'His love has no end.'

I called to the Lord in my distress;
he answered and freed me.
The Lord is at my side; I do not fear.
What can man do against me?
The Lord is at my side as my helper:

It is better to take refuge in the Lord
than to trust in men:
it is better to take refuge in the Lord
than to trust in princes.

I was thrust, thrust down and falling:
but the Lord was my helper.
The Lord is my strength and my song;
he was my saviour.

There are shouts of joy and victory
in the tents of the just.

The Lord's right hand has triumphed;
his right hand raised me up.
The Lord's right hand has triumphed;
I shall not die, I shall live
and recount his deeds.

I was punished, I was punished by the Lord:
but not doomed to die.

Open to me the gates of holiness:
I will enter and give thanks.
This is the Lord's own gate
where the just may enter.
I will thank you for you have given answer
and you are my saviour.

The stone which the builders rejected
has become the corner stone.
This is the work of the Lord,
a marvel in our eyes.
This day was made by the Lord;
we rejoice and are glad.

O Lord, grant us salvation;
O Lord grant success.
Blessed in the name of the Lord
is he who comes.

We bless you from the house of the Lord;
the Lord God is our light.

Go forward in procession with branches
even to the altar.
You are my God, I thank you.
My God I praise you.
Give thanks to the Lord for he is good;
for his love has no end.

118 (119)

1

They are happy whose life is blameless,
who follow God's law!
They are happy those who do his will,
seeking him with all their hearts,
who never do anything evil
but walk in his ways.
You have laid down your precepts
to be obeyed with care.
May my footsteps be firm
to obey your statutes.
Then I shall not be put to shame
as I heed your commands.
I will thank you with an upright heart
as I learn your decrees.
I will obey your statutes:
do not forsake me.

9

How shall the young remain sinless?
By obeying your word.
I have sought you with all my heart:
let me not stray from your commands.
I treasure your promise in my heart
lest I sin against you.
Blessed are you, O Lord;
teach me your statutes.

With my tongue I have recounted
the decrees of your lips.
I rejoiced to do your will
as though all riches were mine.
I will ponder all your precepts
and consider your paths.
I take delight in your statutes,
I will not forget your word.

17
Bless your servant and I shall live
and obey your word.
Open my eyes that I may consider
the wonders of your law.
I am a pilgrim on the earth;
show me your commands.
My soul is ever consumed
in longing for your decrees.
Relieve me from scorn and contempt
for I do your will.
Though princes sit plotting against me
I ponder on your statutes.
Your will is my delight:
your statutes are my counsellors.

25

My soul lies in the dust;
by your word revive me.
I declared my ways and you answered:
teach me your statutes.
Make me grasp the way of your precepts
and I will muse on your wonders.
My soul pines away with grief;
by your word raise me up.
Keep me from the way of error
and teach me your law.
I have chosen the way of truth
with your decrees before me.
I bind myself to do your will;
Lord, do not disappoint me.
I will run the way of your commands;
you give freedom to my heart.

33

Teach me the demands of your statutes
and I will keep them to the end.
Train me to observe your law,
to keep it with my heart.
Guide me in the path of your commands;
for there is my delight.
Bend my heart to your will
and not to love of gain.
Keep my eyes from what is false:
by your word, give me life.

Keep the promise you have made
To the servant who fears you.
Keep me from the scorn I dread,
for your decrees are good,
See, I long for your precepts:
then in your justice, give me life.

41

Lord let your love come upon me,
the saving help of your promise.
And I shall answer those who taunt me:
for I trust in your word.
Do not take the word of truth from my mouth:
for I trust in your decrees.
I shall always keep your law
for ever and ever.
I shall walk in the path of freedom:
for I seek your precepts.
I will speak of your will before kings
and not be abashed.
Your commands have been my delight;
these I have loved.
I will worship your commands and love them
and ponder your statutes.

49

Remember your word to your servant
by which you gave me hope.
This is my comfort in sorrow:

that your promise gives me life,
though the proud may utterly deride me
I keep to your law.
I remember your decrees of old
and these, Lord, console me.
Your statutes have become my song
in the land of exile.
I think of your name in the night-time
and I keep your law.
This has been my blessing,
the keeping of your precepts.

57
My part, I have resolved, O Lord,
is to obey your word.
With all my heart I implore your favour;
show the mercy of your promise.
I have pondered over my ways
and returned to your will.
I made haste and did not delay
to obey your commands.
At midnight I will rise and thank you
for your just decrees.
I am a friend of all who revere you,
who obey your precepts.
Lord, your love fills the earth.
Teach me your statutes.

65

Lord, you have been good to your servant
according to your word.
Teach me discernment and knowledge:
for I trust in your commands.
Before I was afflicted I went astray:
but now I keep your word.
You are good and your deeds are good;
teach me your statutes.
Though proud men smear me with lies
yet I keep your precepts.
Their minds are closed to good
but your law is my delight.
It was good for me to be afflicted,
to learn your statutes.
The law from your mouth means more to me
than silver and gold.

73

It was your hands that made me and shaped me:
help me to learn your commands.
Your faithful will see me and rejoice:
for I trust in your word.
Lord, I know that your decrees are right,
that you afflicted me justly.
Let your love be ready to console me
by your promise to your servant.
Let your love come to me and I shall live:
for your law is my delight.

Let your faithful turn to me,
those who know your will.
Let my heart be blameless in your statutes:
lest I be ashamed.

81
I yearn for your saving help;
I hope in your word.
My eyes yearn to see your promise.
When will you console me?
Though parched and exhausted with waiting
I remember your statutes.
For me the proud have dug pitfalls,
against your law.
Your commands are all true; then help me
when lies oppress me.
They almost made an end of me on earth:
but I kept your precepts.
Because of your love give me life
and I will do your will.

89
Your word, O Lord, for ever
stands firm in the heavens:
your truth lasts from age to age,
like the earth you created.
By your decree it endures to this day;
for all things serve you.
Had your law not been my delight

I would have died in my affliction.
I will never forget your precepts
for with them you give me life.
Save me, for I am yours
since I seek your precepts.
I have seen that all perfection has an end:
but your command is boundless.

97

Lord how I love your law!
It is ever in my mind.
Your command makes me wiser than my foes;
for it is mine for ever.
I have more insight than all who teach me;
for I ponder your will.
I have more understanding than the old;
for I keep your precepts.
I turn my feet from evil paths
to obey your word.
I have not turned away from your decrees;
you yourself have taught me.
Your promise is sweeter to my taste
than honey in the mouth.
I gain understanding from your precepts
and so I hate false ways.

105

Your word is a lamp for my steps
and a light for my path.

I have sworn and have determined
to obey your decrees.
Lord, I am deeply afflicted:
by your word give me life.
Accept, Lord, the homage of my lips
and teach me your decrees.
Though I carry my life in my hands,
I remember your law.
Your will is my heritage for ever,
the joy of my heart.
I set myself to carry out your statutes
in fullness, for ever.

113

I have no love for half-hearted men:
my love is for your law.
You are my shelter, my shield;
I hope in your word.
Leave me, you who do evil;
I will keep God's command.
If you uphold me by your promise I shall live;
let my hopes not be in vain.
Sustain me and I shall be saved
and ever observe your statutes.

121

I have done what is right and just;
let me not be oppressed.
Vouch for the welfare of your servant

lest the proud oppress me.
My eyes yearn for your saving help
and the promise of your justice.
Treat your servant with love
and teach me your statutes.
I am your servant, make me understand;
then I shall know your will.
It is time for the Lord to act
for your law has been broken.
That is why I love your commands
more than finest gold.
That is why I rule my life by your precepts:
I hate false ways.

129

Your will is wonderful indeed;
therefore I obey it.
The unfolding of your word gives light
and teaches the simple.
I open my mouth and I sigh
as I yearn for your commands.
Turn and show me your mercy;
show justice to your friends.
Let my steps be guided by your promise;
let no evil rule me.
Redeem me from man's oppression
and I will keep your precepts.
Let your face shine on your servant
and teach me your decrees.

Tears stream from my eyes
because your law is disobeyed.

137
Lord, you are just indeed;
your decrees are right.
You have imposed your will with justice
and with absolute truth.
Your promise is tried in the fire,
the delight of your servant.
Although I am weak and despised
I remember your precepts.
Your justice is eternal justice
and your law is truth.
Though anguish and distress have seized me,
I delight in your commands.
The justice of your will is eternal:
if you teach me, I shall live.

145
I call with all my heart; Lord, hear me,
I will keep your statutes.
I call upon you, save me
and I will do your will.
I rise before dawn and cry for help,
I hope in your word.
My eyes watch through the night
to ponder your promise.
In your love hear my voice, O Lord;

give me life by your decrees.
Those who harm me unjustly draw near:
they are far from your law.
But you, O Lord, are close:
your commands are truth.
Long have I known that your will
is established for ever.

153

See my affliction and save me:
for I remember your law.
Uphold my cause and defend me;
by your promise, give me life.
Numberless, Lord, are your mercies;
with your decrees give me life.
Though my foes and oppressors are countless
I have not swerved from your will.
See how I love your precepts;
in your mercy give me life.
Your word is founded on truth:
your decrees are eternal.

161

Though princes oppress me without cause
I stand in awe of your word.
I take delight in your promise
like one who finds a treasure.
Lies I hate and detest
But your law is my love.

Seven times a day I praise you
for your just decrees.
The lovers of your law have great peace;
they never stumble.
I await your saving help, O Lord,
I fulfil your commands.
My soul obeys your will
and loves it dearly.
I obey your precepts and your will;
all that I do is before you.

169

Lord, let my cry come before you:
teach me by your word.
Let my pleading come before you;
save me by your promise.
Let my lips proclaim your praise
because you teach me your statutes.
Let my tongue sing your promise
for your commands are just.
Let your hand be ready to help me,
since I have chosen your precepts.
Lord, I long for your saving help
and your law is my delight.
Give life to my soul that I may praise you.
Let your decrees give me help.
I am lost like a sheep; seek your servant:
for I remember your commands.

120 (121)

I lift up my eyes to the mountains:
from where shall come my help?
My help shall come from the Lord
who made heaven and earth.

May he never allow you to stumble!
Let him sleep not, your guard.
No, he sleeps not nor slumbers,
Israel's guard.

The Lord is your guard and your shade;
at your right side he stands.
By day the sun shall not smite you,
nor the moon in the night.

The Lord will guard you from evil,
he will guard your soul.
The Lord will guard your going and coming
both now and for ever.

121 (122)

I rejoiced when I heard them say:
'Let us go to God's house.'
And now our feet are standing
within your gates, O Jerusalem.

Jerusalem is built as a city
strongly compact.
It is there that the tribes go up,
the tribes of the Lord.

For Israel's law it is,
there to praise the Lord's name.
There were set the thrones of judgment
of the house of David.

For the peace of Jerusalem pray:
'Peace be to your homes!
May peace reign in your walls,
in your palaces, peace!'

For love of my brethren and friends
I say: 'Peace upon you!'
For love of the house of the Lord
I will ask for your good.

123 (124)

'If the Lord had not been on our side,'
this is Israel's song.
'If the Lord had not been on our side
when men rose against us,
then would they have swallowed us alive
when their anger was kindled.

'Then would the waters have engulfed us,
the torrent gone over us;
over our head would have swept
the raging waters.'

Blessed be the Lord who did not give us
a prey to their teeth!
Our life, like a bird, has escaped
from the snare of the fowler.

Indeed the snare has been broken
and we have escaped.
Our help is in the name of the Lord,
who made heaven and earth.

124 (125)

Those who put their trust in the Lord
are like Mount Sion, that cannot be shaken,
that stands for ever.

Jerusalem! The mountains surround her,
so the Lord surrounds his people
both now and for ever.

Do good, Lord, to those who are good,
to the upright of heart;

On Israel, peace!

125 (126)

When the Lord delivered Sion from bondage,
it seemed like a dream.
Then was our mouth filled with laughter,
on our lips there were songs.

What marvels the Lord worked for us!
Indeed we were glad.

Deliver us, O Lord, from our bondage
as streams in dry land.
Those who are sowing in tears
will sing when they reap.

They go out, they go out, full of tears,
carrying seed for the sowing:
they come back, they come back, full of song,
carrying their sheaves.

126 (127)

If the Lord does not build the house,
in vain do its builders labour;
if the Lord does not watch over the city,
in vain does the watchman keep vigil.

In vain is your earlier rising,
your going later to rest,
you who toil for the bread you eat:
When he pours gifts on his beloved while they slumber.

127 (128)

O blessed are those who fear the Lord
and walk in his ways!

By the labour of your hands you shall eat.
You will be happy and prosper;

Indeed thus shall be blessed
the man who fears the Lord.
May the Lord bless you from Sion
all the days of your life!

On Israel, peace!

129 (130)

Out of the depths I cry to you, O Lord,
Lord, hear my voice!
O let your ears be attentive
to the voice of my pleading.

If you, O Lord, should mark our guilt,
Lord, who would survive?
But with you is found forgiveness:
for this we revere you.

My soul is waiting for the Lord,
I count on his word.
My soul is longing for the Lord
more than watchmen for daybreak.
(Let the watchman count on daybreak
and Israel on the Lord.)

Because with the Lord there is mercy
and fullness of redemption,
Israel indeed he will redeem
from all its iniquity.

130 (131)

O Lord, my heart is not proud,
nor haughty my eyes.
I have not gone after things too great,
nor marvels beyond me.

Truly I have set my soul
in silence and peace.
A weaned child on its mother's breast,
even so is my soul.

O Israel, hope in the Lord
both now and for ever.

131 (132)

O Lord, remember David
and all the hardships he endured,
the oath he swore to the Lord,
his vow to the Strong One of Jacob.

'I will not enter the house where I live
nor go to the bed where I rest.
I will give no sleep to my eyes,
to my eyelids will give no slumber
till I find a place for the Lord,
a dwelling for the Strong One of Jacob.'

At Ephrata we heard of the ark;
we found it in the plains of Yearim.
'Let us go to the place of his dwelling;
let us go to kneel at his footstool.'

Go up, Lord, to the place of your rest,
you and the ark of your strength.
Your priests shall be clothed with holiness:
your faithful shall ring out their joy.
For the sake of David your servant
do not reject your anointed.

The Lord swore an oath to David;
he will not go back on his word:
'A son, the fruit of your body,
will I set upon your throne.

'If they keep my covenant in truth
and my laws that I have taught them,
their sons also shall rule
on your throne from age to age.'

For the Lord has chosen Sion;
he has desired it for his dwelling;
'This is my resting-place for ever,
here have I chosen to live.

'I will greatly bless her produce,
I will fill her poor with bread.
I will clothe her priests with salvation
and her faithful shall ring out their joy.

'There the stock of David will flower:
I will prepare a lamp for my anointed,
on him my crown shall shine.'

132 & 133 (133 & 134)

How good and how pleasant it is,
brothers dwelling in unity!

It is like the dew of Hermon which falls
on the heights of Sion.
For there the Lord gives his blessing,
life for ever.

O come, bless the Lord,
all you who serve the Lord,
who stand in the house of the Lord,
in the courts of the house of our God.
Lift up your hands to the holy place
and bless the Lord through the night.

May the Lord bless you from Sion,
he who made both heaven and earth.

134 (135)

Alleluia!

Praise the name of the Lord,
praise him, servants of the Lord,
who stand in the house of the Lord
in the courts of the house of our God.

Praise the Lord for the Lord is good.
Sing a psalm to his name for he is loving.
For the Lord has chosen Jacob for himself
and Israel for his own possession.

For I know the Lord is great,
that our Lord is high above all gods.
The Lord does whatever he wills,
in heaven, on earth, in the seas.

He summons clouds from the ends of the earth;
makes lightning produce the rain;
from his treasuries he sends forth the wind.

Lord, your name stands for ever,
unforgotten from age to age:
for the Lord does justice for his people;
the Lord takes pity on his servants.

Sons of Israel, bless the Lord!
Sons of Aaron, bless the Lord!
Sons of Levi, bless the Lord!
You who fear him, bless the Lord!

From Sion may the Lord be blessed,
he who dwells in Jerusalem!

135 (136)

Alleluia!

O give thanks to the Lord for he is good,
for his great love is without end.
Give thanks to the God of gods,
for his great love is without end.
Give thanks to the Lord of lords,
for his great love is without end.

Who alone has wrought marvellous works,
for his great love is without end;
whose wisdom it was made the skies,
for his great love is without end;
who fixed the earth firmly on the seas,
for his great love is without end.

It was he who made the great lights,
for his great love is without end;
the sun to rule in the day,
for his great love is without end;
the moon and stars in the night,
for his great love is without end.

He gives food to all living things,
for his great love is without end;
to the God of heaven give thanks,
for his great love is without end.

137 (138)

I thank you, Lord, with all my heart,
you have heard the words of my mouth.
Before the angels I will bless you.
I will adore before your holy temple.

I thank you for your faithfulness and love
which excel all we ever knew of you.
On the day I called, you answered;
you increased the strength of my soul.

All earth's kings shall thank you
when they hear the words of your mouth.
They shall sing of the Lord's ways:
'How great is the glory of the Lord!'

The Lord is high yet he looks on the lowly;
and the haughty he knows from afar.

You stretch out your hand and save me,
your hand will do all things for me.
Your love, O Lord, is eternal,
discard not the work of your hands.

138 (139)

O Lord, You search me and you know me,
you know my resting and my rising,
you discern my purpose from afar.
You mark when I walk or lie down,
all my ways lie open to you.

Before ever a word is on my tongue
you know it, O Lord, through and through.
Behind and before you besiege me,
your hand ever laid upon me.
Too wonderful for me, this knowledge,
too high, beyond my reach.

O where can I go from your spirit,
or where can I flee from your face?
If I climb the heavens, you are there.
If I lie in the grave, you are there.

If I take the wings of the dawn
and dwell at the sea's furthest end,
even there your hand would lead me,
your right hand would hold me fast.

If I say: 'Let the darkness hide me
and the light around me be night,'
even darkness is not dark for you;
and the night is as clear as the day.

For it was you who created my being,
knit me together in my mother's womb.
I thank you for the wonder of my being,
for the wonders of all your creation.

Already you knew my soul,
my body held no secret from you
when I was being fashioned in secret
and moulded in the depths of the earth.

Your eyes saw all my actions,
they were all of them written in your book;
every one of my days was decreed
before one of them came into being.

To me, how mysterious your thoughts,
the sum of them not to be numbered!
If I count them, they are more than the sand;
to finish, I must be eternal, like you.

O search me, God, and know my heart.
O test me and know my thoughts.
See that I follow not the wrong path
and lead me in the path of life eternal.

140 (141)

I have called to you, Lord; hasten to help me!
Hear my voice when I cry to you.
Let my prayer come before you like incense,
the raising of my hands like an evening oblation.

Lord, set a guard over my mouth;
keep watch at the door of my lips!
Do not turn my heart to things that are wrong.

To you, Lord God, my eyes are turned:
in you I take refuge; spare my soul!
From the trap they have laid for me keep me safe:
keep me from the snares of those who do evil.

141 (142)

With all my voice I cry to the Lord,
with all my voice I entreat the Lord.
I pour out my trouble before him;
I tell him all my distress
while my spirit faints within me.
But you, O Lord, know my path.

On the way where I shall walk
they have hidden a snare to entrap me.
Look on my right and see:
there is not one who takes my part.
I have no means of escape,
not one who cares for my soul.

I cry to you, O Lord.
I have said: 'You are my refuge,
all I have left in the land of the living.'
Listen then to my cry;
For I am in the depths of distress.

Rescue me from those who pursue me;
for they are stronger than I.
Bring my soul out of this prison,
and then I shall praise your name.
Around me the just will assemble
because of your goodness to me.

142 (143)

Lord, listen to my prayer:
turn your ear to my appeal.
You are faithful, you are just; give answer.
Do not call your servant to judgment
for no one is just in your sight.

The enemy pursues my soul;
he has crushed my life to the ground;
he has made me dwell in darkness
like the dead, long forgotten.
Therefore my spirit fails;
my heart is numb within me.

I remember the days that are past:
I ponder all your works.
I muse on what your hand has wrought
and to you I stretch out my hands.
Like a parched land my soul thirsts for you.

Lord, make haste and give me answer;
for my spirit fails within me.
Do not hide your face,
lest I become like those in the grave.

In the morning let me know your love;
for I put my trust in you.
Make me know the way I should walk:
to you I lift up my soul.

Rescue me, Lord, from my enemies;
I have fled to you for refuge.
Teach me to do your will;
for you, O Lord, are my God.
Let your good spirit guide me
in ways that are level and smooth.

For your name's sake, Lord, save my life;
in your justice save my soul from distress.

144 (145)

I will give you glory, O God my King,
I will bless your name for ever.

I will bless you day after day
and praise your name for ever.
The Lord is great, highly to be praised,
his greatness cannot be measured.

Age to age shall proclaim your works,
shall declare your mighty deeds,
shall speak of your splendour and glory,
tell the tale of your wonderful works.

They will speak of your terrible deeds,
recount your greatness and might.
They will recall your abundant goodness;
age to age shall ring out your justice.

The Lord is kind and full of compassion,
slow to anger, abounding in love.
How good is the Lord to all,
compassionate to all his creatures.

All your creatures shall thank you, O Lord,
and your friends shall repeat their blessing.
They shall speak of the glory of your reign
and declare your might, O God,

To make known to men your mighty deeds
and the glorious splendour of your reign.
Yours is an everlasting kingdom;
your rule lasts from age to age.

The Lord is faithful in all his words
and loving in all his deeds.

The Lord supports all who fall
and raises all who are bowed down.

The eyes of all creatures look to you
and you give them their food in due time.
You open wide your hand,
grant the desires of all who live.

The Lord is just in all his ways
and loving in all his deeds.
He is close to all who call him,
who call on him from their hearts.

He grants the desires of those who fear him,
he hears their cry and he saves them.
The Lord protects all who love him.

Let me speak the praise of the Lord,
Let all mankind bless his holy name
for ever, for ages unending.

145 (146)

Alleluia!

My soul, give praise to the Lord;
I will praise the Lord all my days,
make music to my God while I live.

Put no trust in princes,
in mortal men in whom there is no help.
Take their breath, they return to clay
and their plans that day come to nothing.

He is happy who is helped by Jacob's God,
whose hope is in the Lord his God,
who alone made heaven and earth,
the seas and all they contain.

It is he who keeps faith for ever,
who is just to those who are oppressed.
It is he who gives bread to the hungry,
the Lord, who set prisoners free,

The Lord who gives sight to the blind,
who raises up those who are bowed down,
the Lord, who protects the stranger
and upholds the widow and orphan.

It is the Lord who loves the just.
The Lord will reign for ever,
Sion's God, from age to age.

Alleluia!

146 (147A)

Alleluia!

Praise the Lord for he is good;
sing to our God for he is loving:
to him our praise is due.

The Lord builds up Jerusalem
and brings back Israel's exiles,
he heals the broken-hearted,
he binds up all their wounds.
He fixes the number of the stars;
he calls each one by its name.

Our Lord is great and almighty;
his wisdom can never be measured.
The Lord raises the lowly.
Sing to the Lord, giving thanks;
sing psalms to our God with the harp.

He covers the heavens with clouds;
he prepares the rain for the earth,
making mountains sprout with grass
and with plants to serve man's needs.
He provides the beasts with their food
and young ravens that call upon him.

His delight is not in horses
nor his pleasure in warriors' strength.
The Lord delights in those who revere him,
in those who wait for his love.

147 (147B)

O praise the Lord, Jerusalem!
Sion praise your God!

He has strengthened the bars of your gates,
he has blessed the children within you.
He established peace on your borders,
he feeds you with finest wheat.

He sends out his word to the earth
and swiftly runs his command.
He showers down snow white as wool,
he scatters hoar-frost like ashes.

He hurls down hailstones like crumbs.
The waters are frozen at his touch;
he sends forth his word and it melts them:
at the breath of his mouth the waters flow.

He makes his word known to Jacob,
to Israel his laws and decrees.

Alleluia!

148

Alleluia!

Praise the Lord from the heavens:
praise him in the heights.
Praise him, all his angels,
praise him, all his host.

Praise him, sun and moon,
praise him, shining stars.
Praise him, highest heavens,
and the waters above the heavens.

Let them praise the name of the Lord.
He commanded: they were made.
He fixed them for ever,
gave a law which shall not pass away.

Praise the Lord from the earth,
sea creatures and all oceans,
fire and hail, snow and mist,
stormy winds that obey his word;

All mountains and hills,
all fruit trees and cedars,
beasts, wild and tame,
reptiles and birds on the wing;

All earth's kings and peoples,
earth's princes and rulers;
young men and maidens,
old men together with children.

Let them praise the name of the Lord
for he alone is exalted.
The splendour of his name
reaches beyond heaven and earth.

He exalts the strength of his people.
He is the praise of all his saints,
of the sons of Israel,
of the people to whom he comes close.

Alleluia!

149

Alleluia!

Sing a new song to the Lord,
His praise in the assembly of the faithful.
Let Israel rejoice in its Maker,
let Sion's sons exult in their King.
Let them praise his name with dancing
and make music with timbrel and harp.

For the Lord takes delight in his people.
He crowns the poor with salvation.
Let the faithful rejoice in their glory,
shout for joy and take their rest.
Let the praise of God be on their lips.

Alleluia!

150

Alleluia!

Praise God in his holy place,
praise him in his mighty heavens.
Praise him for his powerful deeds,
praise his surpassing greatness.

O praise him with sound of trumpet,
praise him with lute and harp.
Praise him with timbrel and dance,
praise him with strings and pipes.

O praise him with resounding cymbals,
praise him with clashing of cymbals.
Let everything that lives and that breathes
give praise to the Lord. Alleluia!

BEDE GRIFFITHS INTERNATIONAL
CONTEMPLATION CENTRES

Osage Monastery
Sr M Pascaline Coff O.S.B.
18701 W. Monastery Rd.
USA – Sand Springs, OK 74063
Ph: 001–918–245–2734
Fax: 001–918–245–9360

New Camaldoli Hermitage
Fr Robert Hale O.S.B. Cam.
USA – Big Sur, CA 93920
Ph: 001–408–667–0480
Fax: 001–408–667–0480
         (Fr Robert Hale pers.)
         001–408–667–0209
         (Fr Bruno)

Monastero di S. Gregorio Magno
Fr Bernardino Cozzarini O.S.B.
   Cam.
Piazza di S. Gregorio al Celio #1
I–00184 Roma, Italia
Ph: 01139–6–700–8227
Fax: 01139–6–700–9357

Epiphany Monastery
Fr Romuald O.S.B. Cam.
P.O. Box 60
USA – New Boston, NH 03070
Ph: 001–603–487–3020
Fax: 001–603–487–3700

Saccidananda Ashram –
   Shantivanam
Br John Martin Kuvarapu
   O.S.B. Cam.
Tannirpalli 639–107
Kulittalai, Tiruchy Dt.
Tamil Nadu, South INDIA
Ph: 01191–4323–3060
Fax: 01191–4323–4014

Christ by the River Hermitage
Fr Douglas Conlan Obl. O.S.B.
P.O. Box 35
Pinjarra 6208 – W. Australia
Ph: 01161–9–531–1227
Fax: 01161–9–531–2480

Shantigiri/Mount of Peace/
  Berg des Friedens
Roland R. Ropers Obl. O.S.B.
Gräfin-Schlippenbach–Weg 16
D – 83708 Kreuth – Germany
Ph: 01149–8029–8235
        (Clinic)
        01149–8029–8765
        (private)
Fax: 01149–8029–8378
        (Clinic)
        01149–8029–8888
        (personal)

Bede Griffiths International
    Trust Archives
Incarnation Monastery
Br Cassian Hardie O.S.B. Cam.
1369 La Loma
USA – Berkeley, CA 94708
Ph: 001–510–548–0965
Fax: 001–510–845–0601